MY Ai TELLS
"PUNNY JOKES"
And wrote a book about it

Written By:
Chet G. Peety

ISBN: 9798860470743

Cover design by: NEPTAiN Graphics

Printed in the United States of America

PREFACE

The pages that follow in this book were created in their entirety by the language model ChatGPT, developed by OpenAI. Its creative process was directed by human question, however the introductions and jokes you're about to read were created solely from the program itself.

You will notice that the humor varies. While some of the jokes will make you chuckle, others might seem more like simple facts than real jokes. This gives us an interesting look into how the software sees and uses humor, showing us its unique idea of what a 'joke' is.

But this book isn't just about getting laughs. It has a bigger reason, to show the steps we've taken towards not only smart computers, but also machines that might have feelings too. If a computer can get what makes a joke funny and can make up its own funny story, it makes us wonder: does this mean it has some understanding of emotions?

Maybe, in a few years, we'll look back at this book and see it as a cool reminder of how AI started, and how much it has grown since then. This book is a snapshot of an exciting time in the world of Ai. Enjoy

This is only the beginning...

INTRO

Greetings, pun enthusiasts and devotees of double meanings! You're about to navigate a collection custom-tailored for those brief moments of downtime—be it a coffee pause or, candidly, an escape from a to-do list that's lengthier than this book. Each pun you'll encounter is stacked with more nuances than an onion has layers, ready to make you grin, chortle, or even elicit that silent, inward laughter of true understanding.

Now, brace yourself for an unexpected twist. The puns you're about to savor aren't the brainchildren of a seasoned wordsmith or a comedy writer sketching jokes on a cocktail napkin. Instead, they are the algorithmic output of a computer that's been rigorously schooled in the intricacies of human humor. Picture a meeting of the minds between a literary genius and cutting-edge technology; the puns you're about to dive into could very well be the minutes from that extraordinary conference.

You might be pondering, "Sure, I've seen tech perform wonders, but mastering the art of the pun? That's truly next-level!" And you'd be spot on. Consider this volume a comedy club's open mic night, but the machine is the sole act. It's bound to have moments of comedic genius and perhaps a few groan-worthy tries. These are the nuances that remind us how delicate and complex the art of punning is. It's akin to a masterful juggler who manages six balls in the air and then fumbles while taking a bow—both endearing and surprisingly human.

So, what are you waiting for? Flip that page, soak in the first pun, and marvel, "A machine conjured this?" Whether a particular line makes you guffaw, scratch your head, or reevaluate the human condition through the lens of humor, you're not just an audience member. You're a trailblazer in this unexplored realm where silicon circuits try their hand at pun-crafting. Dive in and enjoy the rollercoaster of wordplay, twists, and linguistic acrobatics. The machine sets the stage, but the reactions—the laughs, the groans, the moments of insight—are genuinely yours to experience.

Time flies like an arrow; fruit flies like a banana.

I used to play piano by ear, but now I use my hands. I told my wife she was drawing her eyebrows too high. She looked surprised.

Why did the scarecrow win an award? Because he was outstanding in his field.

I'm reading a book on anti-gravity. It's impossible to put down.

I got a job at a bakery because I kneaded dough. Parallel lines have so much in common. It's a shame they'll never meet.

I used to be a baker, but I couldn't make enough dough.

I told my friend 10 jokes to make him laugh. No pun in ten did.

The mathematician's plants stopped growing, so he found the square root.

I named my dogs Rolex and Timex. They're my watch dogs.

I asked the librarian if the library had books on paranoia. She whispered, "They're right behind you!"

Did you hear about the cheese factory that exploded? There was nothing left but de-brie.

If you see a crime at an Apple Store, does that make you an iWitness?

Why did the bicycle fall over? Because it was two-tired.

I used to play the triangle in a reggae band but I had to quit; it was just one ting after another.
A plateau is the highest form of flattery.

I got kicked out of the karaoke bar last night for singing "Danger Zone" six times in a row. They said I exceeded my maximum number of Loggins attempts.

Never trust an atom. They make up everything! I told my friend I was attacked by an alligator. He said I was in de-Nile.

I'm friends with all electricians. We have good current connections.

What's brown and sticky? A stick! I asked the gym instructor if he could teach me to do the splits. He replied, "How flexible are you?" I said, "I can't make it on Tuesdays."

I told my doctor I broke my arm in two places. He told me to stop going to those places.
How do you catch a squirrel? Climb a tree and act like a nut!

Don't spell part backward. It's a trap.

I have a chicken-proof lawn. It's impeccable.

I used to be addicted to soap, but now I'm clean.

I want to be a baker, but I couldn't raise enough dough.

Why did the golfer bring two pairs of pants? In case he got a hole in one.

I'm reading a book on anti-gravity. It's lifting me up!

I used to be a baker, but I couldn't make enough dough.

Why did the bicycle fall over? Because it was two-tired!

What's a pepper that won't leave you alone? Jalapeño business.

Why was the math book sad? Because it had too many problems.

Why do ducks have feathers? To cover their butt quacks!

What do you call a pile of cats? A meow-tain.

I asked the librarian if the library had books on paranoia. She whispered, "They're right behind you!"

I told my wife she was drawing her eyebrows too high. She looked surprised.

A boiled egg in the morning is hard to beat.

What do you call a fake noodle? An "impasta."

I know a lot of jokes about retired people, but none of them work.

The past, present, and future walked into a bar. It was tense.

The roundest knight at King Arthur's table was Sir Cumference.

When a gardener became a musician, he went from flower beds to head-banging.

When a clock gets hungry, it goes back four seconds.

Never trust a painter; they're always trying to brush you off.

I used to run a dating service for chickens, but I was struggling to make hens meet.

When shoelaces get tired, they just can't "knot."

Tofu never cracks jokes because it doesn't want to be too cheesy.

When an eraser and a pencil fought, it was a draw.

A fish who performs surgery is a sturgeon.

Cowardly veggies never turnip.

Astronauts who misbehave are given a "space-out" time.

A snake's favorite subject is hissss-tory.

Why did the computer cross the road? To get to the other website.

I was struggling to figure out how lightning works, but then it struck me.

Why did the computer take up music? Because it had the right algorithms.

I asked a geologist how her day was, and she said it totally rocked.

My feathered friend can write now; he's a literal bird of a feather.

Spices never win races because they keep getting caught in a jam.

When a tree gets sick, it goes to the root of the problem.

When a pun goes bad, it becomes a "pun-ishment."

My cat wants to be an astronaut. She's already a "space-cadet."

A pessimistic train always thinks it's going off the rails.

Chairs always lose in musical chairs; they can never take a seat.

A pastry chef who steals is a whisk-taker.

Vampires who are bad at math just can't count.

The skittish music note wanted some rest; it was feeling a little flat.

Bread is like the sun; it rises in the yeast and sets in the waist.

The Coffee beans hired security, because they keep getting mugged.

A carpenter's favorite game is "board games."
Why do tech geeks love the beach? Because of all the "sand-bytes."

A theatrical performance about puns is a play on words.

When a fish gets bad grades, it's below sea-level.

A dentist who loves gardening has a lot of root interest.

Lazy kitchen utensils always stir up trouble.

Geese always carry a bill because they never want to be "ducking" out on charges.

Witty cows make moo-vellous puns.

Why did the belt get promoted? Because it held up its end of the bargain.

Ice cream cones make terrible comedians; they always drip their lines.

A clumsy computer always has a bad byte.
A bee who's been rejected from the hive is a free-bee.

Artists always carry sketchy pasts.

Poetic vegetables always have deep roots.

When a window fell in love, it pane-d for its crush.

Old pencils never die; they're just not too sharp anymore.

If you cross a snowman and a dog, you get Frostbite.

How does Moses make his coffee? He brews it.

Candles always get burned out at parties.

The camping trip was in-tents, but nobody got pegged down.

When the sun went to college, it became a little brighter.

Being a locksmith is a key role in society.

Donuts always hole a grudge.

The artist couldn't draw blood because he only dealt with sketchy veins.

The galaxy said to the black hole, "You suck."

Zucchini make terrible detectives; they always squash leads.

The pacifist ghost didn't believe in "boo"-llying.

The shrunken psychic escaped prison, now it's a small, medium, at large

Ice cream scoops always end up in a sundae relationship.

The choir's favorite vegetable was beet-roots; they were pitch-perfect.

A motivational meteor always wants to make an impact.

An acoustic guitar's life is always strung out.

Planets with rings are just heavenly bodies accessorizing.

Archaeologists dig their work but hate being in ruins.

Lizards are great at stand-up; they always "scale" the room first.

A stage actor's favorite fruit is a drama-granate.

Cows don't give milk for free; they're milking the system.

Books can't keep secrets; they always crack open. Dogs who become poets write in "iambic pup-tameter."

Synchronized swimmers never dive-erge.

The claustrophobic astronaut needed more "space."

A musical thief likes to steal the limelight.

Electricians are shocked when they don't conduit right.

A baker's favorite actor is Robert Brownie Jr.

Tires are always going through rough patches.

Helium doesn't react; it's too noble for that.

The bank robber's favorite game was Monopoleave.

Paranoid dice always feel like they're getting rolled.

The best singing vegetables are the rappini.

The baseball team hired a baker because they
needed a good batter.

A spice's favorite band is The Rolling Scones.

A gossipy river never keeps things on the down-low;
it always overflows.

Knights who say jokes always have a pun-in-shining armor.

The ocean says it's not shallow; it has hidden depths.

Ghosts make terrible liars; you can see right through them.

A stressed-out carrot was at its root's end.

Surfer atoms ride the electron wave.

Cardboard boxes always fold under pressure.

Caffeine didn't apply for the job; it was overqualified and overstimulated.

Bad puns are simply tear-able.

Magnets with an attitude have polarity issues.

The gymnast was always flipping out.

The lazy river never flows; it just lounges around.

A cat's favorite game is meow-sical chairs.

Romantic circles always find their center.

Alcoholic pencils always feel "drawn" to the bottle.

Accountants can count on being calculated.

When carrots get into trouble, they always root for each other.

Forks never partake in gossip; they always stick to the point.

Chickens who can't lay eggs are merely "egg-sistential."

Barbers make cutting remarks but always get to the point.

A romantic sailor's love was always in ship-shape. Parrots who gossip are always talking behind your beak.

Philosophical mountains peak too early.

A butterfly's favorite sport is "flutter-by."

Bread puns are the best thing since sliced bread.

Microbes are good at division; they're always multiplying.

The clouds were so lazy they couldn't even form a silver lining.

Philosophical trees always ponder over the root of all knowledge.

Kale never gets invited; it's too chew-dgmental.

Comedians who do gardening always "grow" on you.

A philosopher's favorite drink is "existen-tea."

Unemployed atoms make up everything but contribute nothing.

Pessimistic tires are always feeling flat.

The cube said to the sphere, "Stop going around in circles!"

Parallelograms never get to the point; they're too edgy.

Love-struck doors are always unhinged.

An insecure blanket always felt too "patchy."

Raindrops keep falling on my head, but that's just "water under the bridge."

Suspicious vegetables always "leak" information.

The unprepared rock climber was stuck between a rock and no place.

A smoothie's life is always blended.

The chubby calculator couldn't count its calories.

Zen masters who make tea are steeped in tradition.

An out-of-work jester was nobody's fool.

Emotional puns are a-play on words.

The disgruntled calendar was fed up with its days being numbered.

Nervous watches always have second thoughts.

The light bulb joined a band because it could really "light it up."

A baker's favorite rapper is Bun DMC.

The impatient sand clock was always running out of time.

Quiet pens are always withdrawn but ink deeply.

Pianists have key roles but never lock in on one tune.

Tennis balls are great at service but terrible at holding court.

A karaoke's favorite song is "I Will Always Love Queue."

Sailors who gossip are always fishing for compliments.

The romantic spider said, "Web you marry me?"

An obsessive cleaner always sweeps off their feet.

Watermelons never fight; they hash it out peacefully.

A banjo's life always strings along.

Chess pieces never keep secrets; it's always a game of "tell."

Sentimental potatoes are full of "mash-y" feelings.

A goofy octopus always cracks tentac-jokes.

The lawyer's pants were always in a "brief."

A psychologist's favorite snack is Freud chicken.

A mathematician's plants stopped growing, so he found the square root of the problem

A horse is a very stable animal.

The kleptomaniac didn't understand any of the puns, he took everything literally.

A chicken crossing the road is poultry in motion.

If you put your money in the blender, you'll have liquid assets.

A bicycle can't stand on its own because it's two-tired.

When a calf is born, it's de-calf-inated.

When the electricity went off during a storm, I was delighted.

When the fog lifted, it mist everyone.

My dog gave birth to puppies near the road and was cited for littering.

If a judge is just, then is a thief taking things justly?

I know sign language, it's pretty handy.

You can tune a guitar, but you can't tuna fish.

The pun is mightier than the sword.

A pessimist's blood type is always b-negative.

Mathematicians have problems, but they know how to solve them.

Astronomers got tired of watching the moon go around the Earth for 24 hours, so they just called it a day.

The shoemaker did not deny his apprentice anything he needed. He gave his awl.

My friend wanted to become an archaeologist, but I tried to put him off. I knew he would get buried in his work.

I know a guy who collects candy canes; they are all in mint condition.

When a gardener feels down, he gets to the root of the problem.

Architects always have concrete plans.

Old electricians never die; they just lose their spark.

Drones that lose their way suffer from "Buzz-orientation."

A fish that studies for tests is good at "scale-matics."

When the calendar factory burned down, all its days were numbered.

I used to be a watchmaker, but I couldn't find the time.

The sea is so friendly; it always waves.

The pensive cannon thought it was always getting fired.

An arrogant rabbit is a hare that doesn't care.

If you steal someone's coffee, is it called "mugging"?

Owls always think ahead; they're known for being pre-meditative.

The agitated wind said it was just blowing off steam.

The book on anti-gravity is impossible to put down.

When you dream in color, it's a pigment of your imagination.

If you don't pay your exorcist, you get repossessed.

A butcher who's good at his job is a cut above the rest.

When the bicycle met the motorcycle, they found they had a wheel-y great connection.

I named my dog "Five Miles" so I can say I walk Five Miles every day.

Mathematicians are sum-bodies, too.

Unemployed jokers are no laughing matter.

Did you hear about the circus fire? It was in-tents.

The satellite fell in love with a planet, and they had a heavenly body.

The rolling pin was on a roll in the kitchen.

Lawyers always wear suits because they're so accustomed to "brief" appearances.

A pessimist's blood type is always b-negative.

Optometrists live life in a lens of possibilities.

Archaeologists dig up the past but have little to urn.

Cows have hooves because they lactose.

A flashlight is a case for holding dead batteries.

Bakers knead dough to get bread, but they also need bread to get dough.

Sheep are great at wool-gathering but terrible at follow-through.

Locksmiths make great comedians; they always have the "key" to humor.

The moon landing was stellar, but Neil Armstrong's pun was "one giant leap" ahead.

When the iPhone broke, it had a "touching" farewell. Weightlifters make terrible musicians; they can't find the right "tone."

Glassblowers have fragile egos; they shatter easily.

Mathematicians are great at dividing their attention but terrible at subtracting their problems.

Gardeners have the best thyme but often find themselves in the weeds.

Batteries were the most charged participants in the electronics meeting.

A firefly's love life is simply electrifying.

A backward poet writes inverse.

I have a friend who's a baker. He kneads the dough.

The circle was self-centered but well-rounded.

When the filmmaker went broke, he couldn't make "cents" of it.

The chiropractor had a backbone for business.

When pencils vowed to stop breaking, it was a point well made.

The exhausted worker became a shell of a man, tirelessly running on empty.

Vampire novels always suck the life out of me.

The astronaut broke up with his girlfriend because he needed more "space."

The wind turbine was a huge fan of renewable energy.

The elevator joke was uplifting, but the escalator one was a real letdown.

The credit card felt maxed out and needed some balance in life.

The belt was tight but always held it together.

A tennis player's favorite city is Volleywood.

A dentist's favorite hymn is "Crown Him with Many Crowns."

The plagiarist was so unoriginal, he even copied this pun.

The guy who invented the door knocker got a "No-bell" prize.

The lumberjack couldn't hack it, so he got the axe.

The optometrist fell into a lens grinder and made a spectacle of himself.

The piano tuner's job was key to harmony.

When geese get sick, they have to go to the duck-tor.

A haunted house for sale was looking for new "boo-yers."

A bank manager without anyone around is a "loan-ly" person.

The guy who invented the snooze button is not very alarming.

What's a composer's favorite game? Haydn seek.

The smog lifted in Los Angeles, and UCLA.

Don't spell part backward. It's a trap.

The theoretical physicist got a job at a soap bubble factory: He was an expert in surface tension.

The guy who invented Velcro got stuck with his idea.

The train track thought it was always being railroaded.

Have you heard about the magic tractor? It turned into a field.

The office chair felt it was always being pushed around.

An egg getting beat felt totally "whipped."

The one who stole my soap is a dirty thief.

The taxidermist had a stuffy personality.

"Parasites" were a real louse-y subject for biologists.

The vacuum cleaner complained about its job sucking.

A dentist's favorite game is "caps and crowns."

Have you heard about the musical gardener? He was great with compost-itions.

Diarrhea is hereditary; it runs in your jeans.

The calendar wanted a day off but was overbooked.

What did the big flower say to the little flower?
"Hey, bud!"

No one liked the origami teacher; she always folded under pressure.

A nervous needle always gets to the point.

When an artist couldn't finish their painting, they were "canvas-tipated."

Writers who become too attached to their work suffer from "pen-dency."

What do you call a group of musical whales? An orca-stra.

Don't read the book on anti-gravity, it's uplifting.

The fork got into a fight; it was a utensil war.

The gossipy garden tools were known to rake over the old leaves.

What did the shy pebble wish? That it was a little bolder.

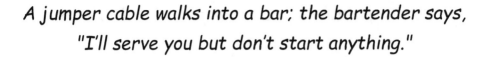

A jumper cable walks into a bar; the bartender says, "I'll serve you but don't start anything."

What's a teacher's favorite nation? Expla-nation.

Did you hear about the guy who got hit in the head with a can of soda? He was lucky it was a soft drink.

Sausages always feel like they're being grilled.

What did one wall say to the other wall? "I'll meet you at the corner."

The locksmith always keyed into conversations.

"You're pointless," said the pencil to the eraser.

What do you call a shoe made of a banana? A slipper!

The procrastinating rock just couldn't get rolling..

The watch was a real attention seeker; it always wanted to be wound up.

When a tree fell in the forest, it couldn't get up because it was "timber!"

The surgeon really knew how to "cut up."

What did the man say when he walked into the bar?
"Ouch."

The cat said it was tired because it had been
"running around all day."

What did the left eye say to the right eye?
"Between you and me, something smells."

Failed magicians are known to "disappear" into
obscurity.

A pessimistic shovel always thought it was getting
"dumped on."

A group of musical notes that stick together is a "chord family."

People who steal ore are boulder than most.

The frustrated sun clock decided it was time to throw in the towel.

When the math book lost its appendix, it had a problem set removed.

What do you call a snowman with a six-pack? An abdominal snowman.

The piece of string said it was always getting "tied up" at work.

Geologists don't take their jobs for granite.

The coin was always "cents-itive" about change.

The fisherman had a net income but had trouble keeping it afloat.

Spiders are great web designers.

What do you call a crate of ducks? A box of quackers.

"Lettuce romaine friends," said the salad.

The sausage declared, "I'm link-ed to great taste!"

The thunder was under the weather; it couldn't break the stormy mood.

The frustrated eraser always felt rubbed the wrong way.

The river felt it had too many mouths to feed; it was estuaries old.

What did the rug say to the floor? "I got this covered!"

When the sugar ran out, it felt "refined" no more.

The introverted flower kept to its bud.

The detective used concrete evidence to cement his case.

Ghosts make terrible comedians; they can't keep a straight face.

The film editor was always cutting corners.

The lightning was flashy but had no real spark.

The quiet mummy had a lot wrapped up inside.

The star at the theater was a real "shoe-in."

The loose screw felt it had lost its grip on life.

The cat who ate too much yarn gave birth to mittens.

The stressed gardener lost his patients but kept his perennials.

The witty hen laid "deviled" eggs.

The lazy river never went with the flow.

The clumsy skydiver had a falling out with gravity.

"You're brewing up trouble," the coffee told the sugar.

What did the man say when he lost all his tools? "I've lost my hardware, but I still have my software."

The dissatisfied mirror always felt it was reflecting poorly

When the volcano met the sea, it said, "You melt my heart."

The train was on the right track, but it had too much emotional baggage.

Why was the triangle so calm? Because it was never bent out of shape.

What did the hungry book say? "I could eat a paragraph."

The moon couldn't attend the sun's party because it needed space.

The badminton birdie said, "I'm always getting batted around."

Why did the musician break up with his metronome? It couldn't keep up.

Why did the opera singer go to jail? Because she broke too many glasses.

What did one sock say to the missing sock? "You complete me."

"I've got a steep learning curve," said the cliff to the mountain.

The alphabet was thrown into jail because it was always up to no good from A to Z.

"You're so dramatic," said the theater to the film.

"My life is a total wreck," said the ship to the iceberg.

What did the clock say when it was hungry? "Is it time to eat yet?"

The introverted hat said, "I'm just not a fan of heads."

"You always make me lose my temper," said the furnace to the vent.

What did the keys say to the piano? "You strike a chord with me."

The frog was down on its luck; it was always in a lily pad mood.

Why did the candle get kicked out of school? Because it was always burning out.

Why was the belt arrested? For holding up a pair of pants.

"You're such a drip," the faucet told the sink.

The architect was well-structured, but his life was a blueprint for chaos.

"You're always buzzing around," said the flower to the bee.

The wall said to the graffiti, "You've really made your mark on me."

What did the squirrel give his wife? "Acorn-y" love letter.

"You're so annoying," said the static to the radio.

What did the paper say to the pencil? "You dot my i's."

The struggling vine finally found something to cling to.

The archeologist had an old-school approach, digging up the past.

When it comes to fixing air conditioners, technicians have their fans.

What did the baker give his wife for Valentine's Day? A bunch of "flours."

The mountain's autobiography was filled with peaks and valleys.

The fish who became a musician was really good with the bass.

"Don't be so negative," said the proton to the electron.

What's a construction worker's favorite game?
"Build or no build."

The poor sock felt "defeeted" when it couldn't find its pair.

To the chagrin of their parents, the teenage magnets were always repelling authority.

The bread was getting stale and needed a fresh start.

The lemon found itself in a bit of a squeeze.

The yoga instructor was always a bit of a stretch.

The grapefruit felt a bit sour about life.

The chef's knife had a cutting edge.

The embarrassed sweater was unraveled by the situation.

The salt was a seasoned veteran.

The frustrated soup was always getting steamed.

The pebble wanted to become a boulder, but it wasn't taken for granite.

The sunflower turned toward new opportunities.

What do you call a well-dressed lion? Dandy-lion.

The diligent hammer felt it nailed its responsibilities.

"You're brew-tiful," said the coffee to the mug.

The struggling clock was always facing time constraints.

The somber window felt pane-fully transparent.

The wandering apostrophe was possessive about its space.

The olive wanted peace but found itself in a pickle.

The sassy scissors were always cutting remarks.

What did the pavement say to the road? "You always lead me on

"Don't sugarcoat it," said the doughnut to the baker, "I'm already sweet enough as is!"

CONCLUSION

Well, here we are, standing at the edge of this delightful rabbit hole we've traveled together—our journey through puns, double meanings, and linguistic curiosities is reaching its finale. Whether you used this book as your go-to procrastination tool or as a mental gym for your wit, we hope it has been as entertaining for you to read as it has been groundbreaking for a machine to compose.

Did you ever pause to consider that this might be a watershed moment? A point in history where humor—once considered the exclusive domain of human creativity—is shared with the algorithmic intellect of a machine? These puns might not all be home runs, but remember, even Babe Ruth struck out sometimes. And in this case, the 'Babe Ruth' is a computer, the ballpark is your mind, and the ball—well, that's your sense of humor, and it's still soaring.

If you've found yourself laughing out loud, chuckling quietly, or even just enjoying a solitary grin, then this compilation has done its job. And if some of the puns had you scratching your head or groaning audibly, that's just a testament to the unpredictable nature of humor. After all, a pun that falls flat only reminds us how incredibly intricate and delightful our language can be, filled with multiple meanings and endless possibilities for interpretation.

As you close this book and step back into your daily life, take with you not just the puns but the marvel of what has been attempted here: a fusion of human wit and mechanical capability. You were not just a passive reader; you were an active participant in an unprecedented experiment where silicon aspired to tickle the human soul.

Thank you for joining us on this unparalleled escapade of wordplay and wisdom. Remember, the machine provided the material, but the laughter, the smiles, and yes, even the groans, are entirely your own. Until we meet again in the ever-expanding realm of puns, keep those wits sharp and that humor flowing.

01010100

01101000

01100101

00100000

01000101

01101110

01100100

ENJOYED THIS BOOK ?
SCAN THE QR CODE TO EXPLORE MORE FROM
CHET G. PEETY